Early
TRANSPORTATION
Encyclopedias

MOTORCYLES

by Deborah A. Rogus

Early Encyclopedias

An Imprint of Abdo Reference
abdobooks.com

abdobooks.com

Published by Abdo Reference, a division of ABDO, PO Box 398166, Minneapolis, Minnesota 55439. Copyright © 2024 by Abdo Consulting Group, Inc. International copyrights reserved in all countries. No part of this book may be reproduced in any form without written permission from the publisher. Early Encyclopedias™ is a trademark and logo of Abdo Reference.

Printed in China
102023
012024

Editor: Carrie Hasler
Series Designer: Candice Keimig

Publisher's Cataloging-in-Publication Data

Library of Congress Control Number: 2023939670

Names: Rogus, Deborah A., author.
Title: Motorcycles / by Deborah A. Rogus
Description: Minneapolis, Minnesota : Abdo Reference, 2024 | Series: Early transportation
     encyclopedias | Includes online resources and index.
Identifiers: ISBN 9781098292928 (lib. bdg.) | ISBN 9798384910862 (ebook)
Subjects: LCSH: Motorcycles--Juvenile literature. | Motorcycling--Juvenile literature. | Motorcycles--
     History--Juvenile literature. | Vehicles--Juvenile literature. | Transportation--Juvenile literature. |
     Encyclopedias and dictionaries--Juvenile literature.
Classification: DDC 629.224--dc23

CONTENTS

Let's Take a Ride!

Motorcycles take people from place to place. They are like bicycles. In fact, the first motorcycle started as a bicycle. A motor was attached to make it go faster.

But motorcycles are faster, heavier, and bigger than bicycles. The frame is made of steel. There are a lot of parts that make a motorcycle work. Motorcycles are used for racing or doing tricks. They can be driven just for fun. Motorcycles can also help people do their jobs.

Some people like to fix up old bikes. Other people like to customize bikes. Many riders go to motorcycle races and rallies. There is so much to discover!

How Motorcycles Work

Most motorcycles have a gas engine. A mix of gas and air enters the engine. With a spark, the gas and air make a small explosion. The explosion pushes a piston. The piston moves up and down. It is connected to engine parts. These parts spin the back wheel.

Windscreen
Handgrip:
twists to give
the engine power
Lever:
squeezes to stop
the front wheel
Headlight
Fuel Tank
Seat
Engine
Foot Pedal:
stops the back
wheel

1884: The first motorcycle was built by Edward Butler in Great Britain. It had three wheels!

1885: Daimler Reitwagen was the first gas-powered motorcycle. The engine was called the grandfather clock.

1901: Indian Motocycle Company was formed in Massachusetts.

1903: Harley-Davidson Company was formed in Wisconsin.

1907: The first Tourist Trophy motorcycle race was held.

1916: The Harley-Davidson J motorcycle was used in World War I (1914–1918).

1938: The first Black Hills Classic rally race was held in Sturgis, South Dakota. ———

1942: The Indian Model 741 was built to be used in World War II (1939–1945).

1988: The first Superbike World Championship was held.

2010: Rocky Robinson set a new speed record at 376 miles per hour (605 kmh) riding a custom bike called the TOP 1 Ack Attack.

Legends Of the Road

Some motorcycles have become famous. They may have a special design. Or they were used for a special purpose. Others have been around for a long time. Some people like to buy old motorcycles and fix them up. These special motorcycles are called classics.

BMW R32

Years Made:
1923 to1926

Maximum Horsepower (Hp):
8.5 hp (1923 model)

Top Speed:
59 mph
(95 kmh), (1923 model)

Weight:
268 pounds
(122 kg), (1923 model)

Did You Know?

Horsepower is a way to talk about the power of an engine. A long time ago, horses were used to pull things. People compared engines to horses. A motorcycle with a high horsepower means it is powerful.

This bike was first shown in Germany. The R32 was a huge success. People loved the design. It was also built well.

Harley-Davidson's WWI and WWII Motorcycles

Harley-Davidson made motorcycles for World War I and World War II. The US Army and its allies used the bikes. The bikes helped deliver messages. They also carried medical supplies. Some carried bullets to the front line.

Harley-Davidson J Motorcycle

The J motorcycle was built for World War I (1914–1918). Some motorcycles had a sidecar. The bikes could carry passengers. Other bikes had machine guns mounted to them. All of the J motorcycles were painted olive green.

Years Made:
1914 to 1918

Top Speed:
85 mph
(137 kmh), (1914 model)

Weight:
325 pounds
(147 kg), (1914 model)

Maximum Hp:
18 hp (1914 model)

FUN FACT!

After World War I, the army sold the leftover bikes to police departments.

Harley-Davidson WLA

During World War II (1939–1945), Harley-Davidson made nearly 90,000 WLA bikes. They carried messages and supplies.

Harley-Davidson began making the WLA again when the Korean War started.

FUN FACT!

Many returning World War II soldiers bought WLAs.

Harley-Davidson made a sidecar in 1914. It was first used by the US Army in 1916. The sidecar carried army supplies.

Years Made:
1940 to 1945; 1949 to 1952

Maximum Hp:
23.5 hp (1942 model)

Top Speed:
65 mph
(105 kmh), (1942 model)

Weight:
576 pounds
(261 kg), (1942 model)

Harley-Davidson XR750

The XR750 was a new kind of dirt bike. It was made for racing. It has won more dirt bike races than any other bike.

It has also been used for stunts. Famous stunt rider Evel Knievel rode this bike! One of his most famous jumps was over 13 Greyhound buses!

FUN FACT!

Evel Knievel's bike was red, white, and blue. And so was his jumpsuit!

Years Made:
1970 to 1980

Maximum Hp:
81.8 hp (1970 model)

Top Speed:
145 mph
(233 kmh), (1970 model)

Weight:
320 pounds
(145 kg), (1970 model)

Did You Know?

Evel Knievel was a daredevil. He jumped motorcycles in the 1960s and 1970s. Many of his famous jumps were made on a 1972 Harley-Davidson XR750.

Honda CB750

The CB750 had a lot of power. It became an instant hit. It is called the godfather of the modern superbikes.

The bike was reliable. That means it didn't break down. It was also easy to customize.

Years Made:
1969 to 2003; 2007

Maximum Hp:
67 hp (1969 model)

Top Speed:
123 mph
(198 kmh), (1969 model)

Weight:
499 pounds (226 kg), (1969 model)

Honda Super Hawk

Robert Pirsig and his son drove from Minnesota to California and back. They rode the Honda Super Hawk. After his trip, Pirsig wrote a book. It was called *Zen and the Art of Motorcycle Maintenance: An Inquiry into Values*. The book became a bestseller.

Years Made:
1961 to 1967

Maximum Hp:
28 hp (1961 model)

Top Speed:
100 mph
(161 kmh), (1961 model)

Weight:
351 pounds
(159 kg), (1961 model)

FUN FACT!

The bike is on display at the Smithsonian's National Museum of American History.

Indian Chief Motorcycle

This motorcycle has an image of an American Indian head on its fender. Others had the word *Indian* painted on them. Many had an Indian head painted on the tank.

The Indian Chief motorcycle is on display at the Smithsonian's National Museum of the American Indian.

1946 Indian Chief

Years Made:
1922 to1953; 1999 to present

Maximum Hp:
40 hp (1947 model)

Top Speed:
85 mph
(137 kmh), (1947 model)

Weight:
550 pounds
(249 kg), (1947 model)

Did You Know?
George M. Hendee and Oscar Hedstrom started the Indian Motocycle Company. Their first motorcycle sold in 1902. In 1920, the Indian Scout motorcycle was built. In 1923, the company's name became Indian Motorcycle.

Norton Manx

The Norton Manx had a light frame. It was called the featherbed frame. It made the bike faster and easier to ride. Other motorcycle companies copied this design.

Did You Know?

The Isle of Man is a small island. It is between England and Ireland. Every year, motorcycles race there. It is called the Isle of Man Tourist Trophy race.

Years Made:
1947 to 1962

Maximum Hp:
45 hp (1949 model)

Top Speed:
108 mph
(174 kmh), (1949 model)

Weight:
330 pounds
(150 kg), (1949 model)

FUN FACT!
The first Isle of Man Tourist Trophy race was held in 1907.

Triumph Bonneville T120

Years Made:
1959 to 1974

Maximum Hp:
46 hp (1962 model)

Top Speed:
110 mph
(177 kmh), (1962 model)

Weight:
393 pounds
(178 kg), (1962 model)

Did You Know?

The Bonneville Salt Flats are flat and all white. Why? The ground is covered in salt! It used to be a lake. But the lake dried up. The salt was left behind.

The Bonneville is named after the Bonneville Motorcycle Speed Trials. The races take place in the Bonneville Salt Flats in Utah. This motorcycle is one of Britain's fastest and most famous bikes. A new version of this bike is still being made today.

The Bonneville Motorcycle Speed Trials is an event that happens every year. Many speed records are set at the races.

Vincent Black Shadow

The Vincent Black Shadow was fast. It was the fastest bike for 25 years. In 1973, the Kawasaki Z1900 broke the Vincent Black Shadow's top speed by going 132 mph (212 kmh).

Years Made:
1948 to 1954

Maximum Hp:
55 hp (1950 model)

Top Speed:
125 mph
(201 kmh), (1950 model)

Weight:
500 pounds
(227 kg), (1950 model)

All Vincent bikes were handmade. They looked like works of art. People thought they looked futuristic. They have been in movies.

FUN FACT!

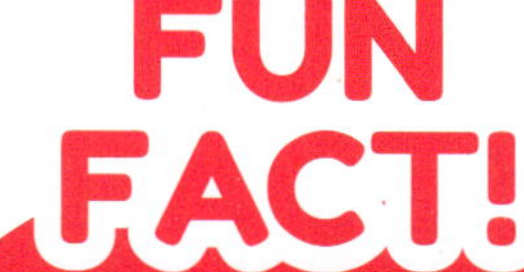

The Black Shadow was the world's first superbike. Superbikes are built to go super fast!

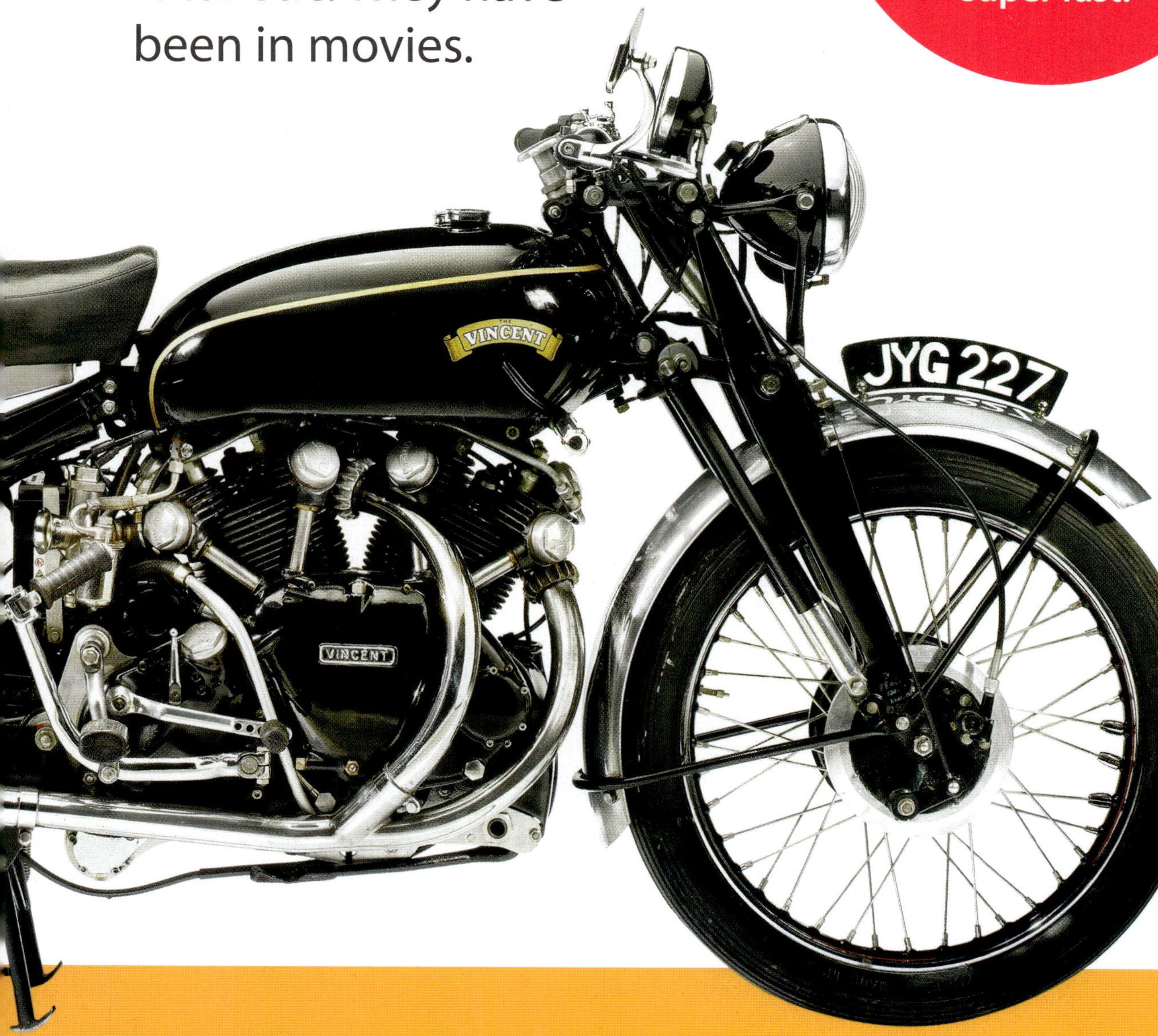

Buell XB12R Firebolt

Erik Buell once worked for Harley-Davidson. He left the company in 1983 and started Buell Motorcycles. The Firebolt was built from 2003 to 2007.

Harley-Davidson F

The F Model was built from 1914 to 1929. This bike made Harley-Davidson famous.

Harley-Davidson Sportster

Production began on the Sportster in 1957. Because the bike was lightweight and had a lower seat, it was popular with female riders.

Kawasaki Z1

The Z1 was built from 1972 to 1975. It is nicknamed the "New York Steak." Why? Many people think a New York steak is the best kind of steak.

Adventure on Two Wheels

A dual-purpose motorcycle can be driven on two places: on the road and off the road. Why would riders want a dual-purpose bike? They can hop on their bikes and ride to a dirt road. Then they can enjoy the adventure.

These bikes have been around a long time. The first motorcycle was dual-purpose. Why? Many towns still had dirt roads.

Tracker

FUN FACT!

The word *dual* means "two."

Scrambler

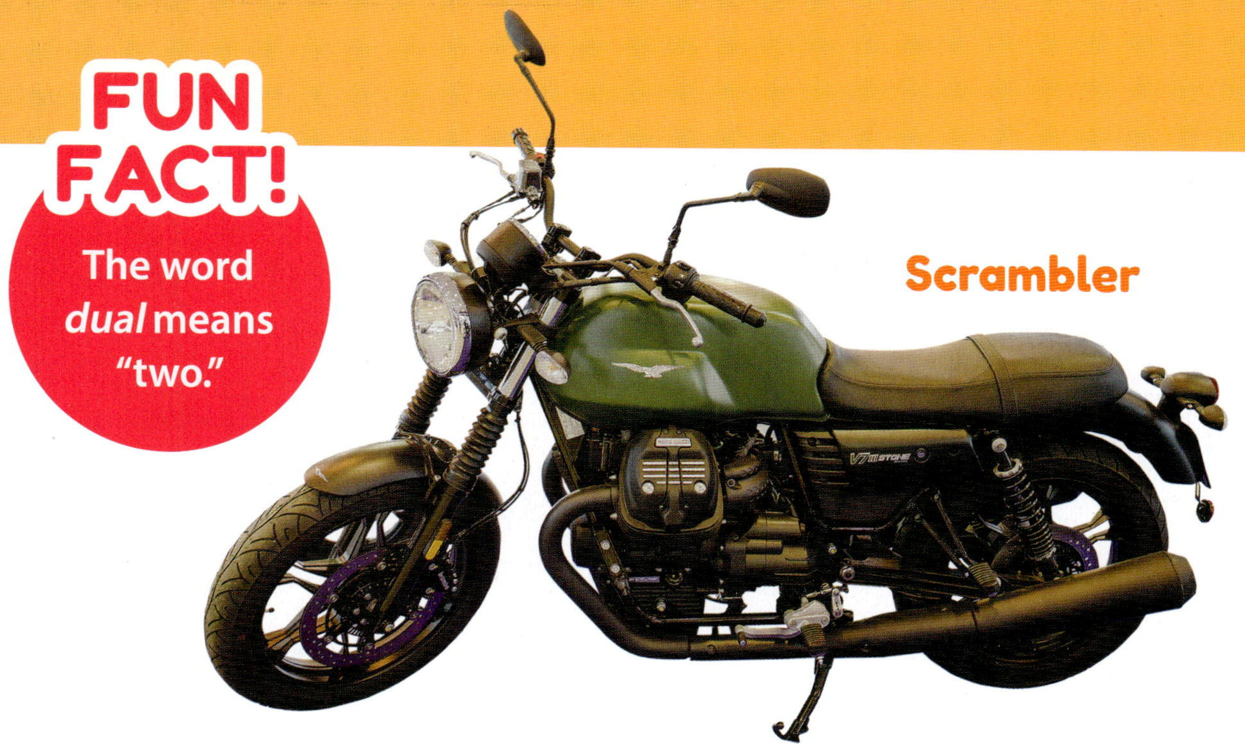

The most popular dual-purpose bike is the adventure bike. Trackers and scramblers are also popular.

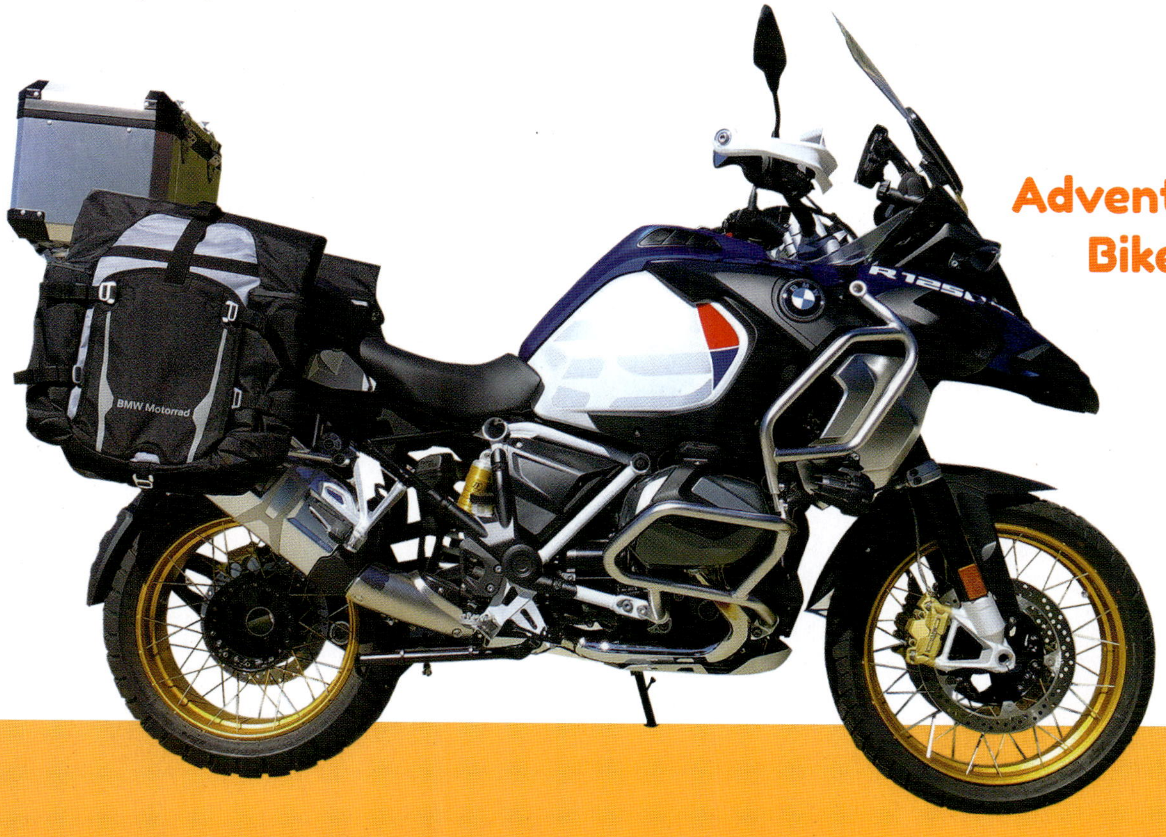

Adventure Bike

Adventure Bikes

Adventure bikes ride well off-road. But they drive better on the road. They are good for long-distance rides. They have a windscreen and padded seat. They also have storage space and a large gas tank. Their tires are made for the pavement.

BMW R80G/S

The BMW R80G/S was one of the first adventure bikes made. It was perfect for riders who wanted to travel and explore. They could ride in comfort and then take their bikes off-road. When this bike came out, other motorcycle makers began making adventure bikes.

FUN FACT!

This bike's engine was called an "airhead." It was cooled by air.

Years Made:
1980 to 1987

Maximum Hp:
50 hp (1985 model)

Top Speed:
104 mph
(167 kmh), (1985 model)

Weight:
410 pounds
(186 kg), (1985 model)

Did You Know?

What's the difference between a dual-sport and an adventure bike? Dual-sport bikes are dirt bikes that can be driven on the street. Adventure bikes are road bikes that can be driven in the dirt. They are faster and are more comfortable than dual-sport bikes.

Scramblers

Like adventure bikes, scramblers ride better on the road. But they still drive well off-road. They have a high ground clearance. They can go over small rocks and bumps without getting stuck.

Did You Know?

A long time ago, bikers would take all the extra parts off their motorcycles. This made them lighter and faster. Then the bikers entered short races called scramblers. That's how the bike got its name!

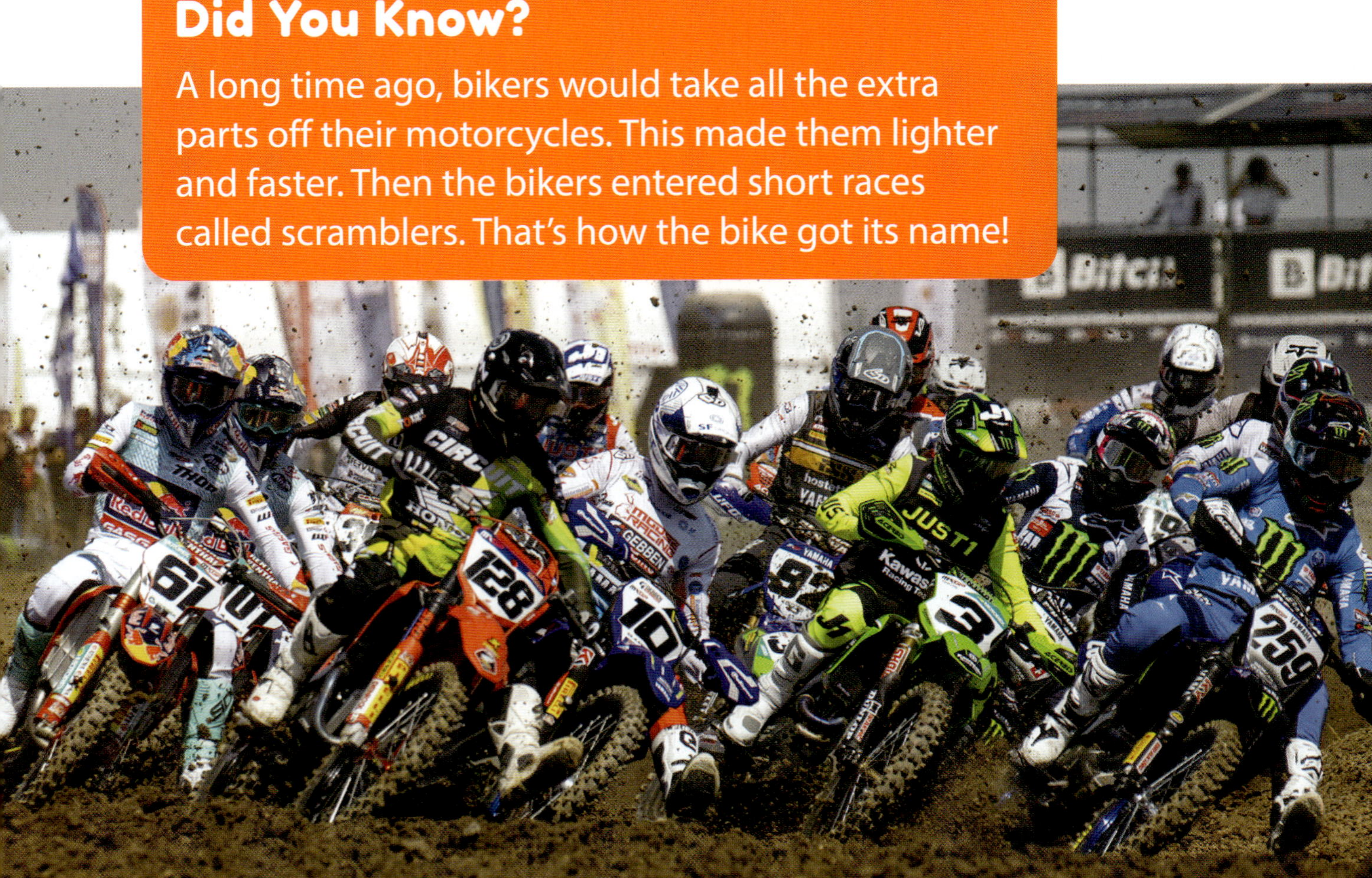

Triumph Street Scrambler 900

Scramblers, like the Triumph Street Scrambler 900, have a simple design. They have a smaller fuel tank and seat. The design makes them weigh less. That makes them easier to ride.

Years Made:
2006 to 2016

Maximum Hp:
59 hp (2016 model)

Top Speed:
104 mph
(167 kmh), (2016 model)

Weight:
471 pounds
(214 kg), (2016 model)

Trackers

Bikers can ride trackers on and off the road. But some trackers never see the dirt. Trackers were made for flat-track racing. A flat track is a large oval track. It is completely flat.

Trackers have long seats. The seats curve up at the end. This helps keep racers on the bike. Trackers have handlebars like dirt bikes.

Did You Know?

Super Hooligan racing is done on a flat track. The goal is to go as fast as possible. The bikes have little to no customization. Fans like this. The bikes are like the ones they ride.

Harley-Davidson Street 750

Harley-Davidson helped grow flat-track racing. It became an official sport at the Summer X Games.

Years Made:
2015 to 2021

Maximum Hp:
57 hp (2015 model)

Top Speed:
105 mph
(169 kmh), (2015 model)

Weight:
503 pounds
(228 kg), (2015 model)

AMPED UP!

Electric motorcycles are powered by electricity. They use a battery instead of gas.

Electric bikes do not make air pollution. They can be better for the planet. But they may not be the best for traveling long distances. The battery cannot go many miles on one charge.

BMW CE 04

The BMW CE 04 rides low to the ground. This makes it handle well on the road.

Years Made:
2021 to present

Maximum Hp:
42 hp (2023 model)

Top Speed:
75 mph
(121 kmh), (2023 model)

Range on One Charge:
80 miles
(129 km), (2023 model)

Weight:
509 pounds
(231 kg), (2023 model)

Lightning LS-218 Electric Superbike

The Lightning has been built since 2014. It's meant to go fast— like lightning!

Super Soco TC

The Super Soco TC is like an electric moped. Owners don't need a motorcycle license to ride it.

Zero FX

The Zero FX is a sports bike. It is made from the same metal that is used for making airplanes. The Zero FX is comfortable enough to drive around town. It's also good on trails.

PLAYING IN THE DIRT

Off-road motorcycles are also known as dirt bikes. They can drive in the dirt and on grass. They can drive across rocks. They can go over bumps without a problem.

FUN FACT!

It is illegal, or against the law, to drive off-road motorcycles on a street.

Dirt bikes are built for fun and adventure. They're also for tricks and racing. Enduros, supermotos, and trials bikes are all off-road bikes.

Did You Know?

In motocross, riders race over rough terrain. The courses are 1 to 3 miles (1.6 to 4.8 km) long. Some parts are wet. Some are dry. All courses have different types of jumps. No two courses are alike. That makes motocross challenging. Riders don't know what to expect!

Dirt Bikes

Dirt bikes are meant for what their name says: dirt! The seat on a dirt bike is higher than on a street bike.

Dirt bikes weigh less than street bikes. That makes them easier to handle. It also makes it easier to do jumps.

Honda CRF250R

Racer Jett Lawrence rode the CRF250R. He won many races with it. He won the 250 East Supercross in 2023. He also won two AMA Motocross National Championships.

FUN FACT!

Bumps on the tires give dirt bikes more traction.

Years Made:
2004 to present

Maximum Hp:
37.6 hp (2022 model)

Top Speed:
70 mph
(113 kmh), (2022 model)

Weight:
229 pounds
(104 kg), (2022 model)

Suzuki RM125

The RM125 is powerful. That makes it harder to control. It may not be a good choice for beginners. But it is a popular bike for motocross racers.

Years Made:
1975 to 2008

Maximum Hp:
38 hp (2001 model)

Top Speed:
65 mph
(105 kmh), (2001 model)

Weight:
192 pounds
(87 kg), (2001 model)

Yamaha YZ250

The YZ250 was the first bike to use a monoshock. This made it more comfortable and drive smoother.

Holes were drilled into parts of the YZ250's frame. The holes made the bike weigh less. That meant the bike could go faster!

Years Made:
1974 to present

Maximum Hp:
20 hp (1974 model)

Top Speed:
85 mph
(137 kmh), (1974 model)

Weight:
245 pounds
(111 kg), (1974 model)

Enduro and Dual-Sport Motorcycles

Enduro motorcycles are a type of dirt bike. They are made for long endurance races. That's where the name *enduro* comes from. Riders are not allowed to drive them on the street.

Honda Dual-Sport CRF300L

Dual-sport bikes, like the Honda Dual-Sport CRF300L, are enduro bikes that have been customized. Dual-sport bikes can drive on the street.

Years Made:
2020 to present

Maximum Hp:
27.3 hp (2021 model)

Top Speed:
80 mph
(129 kmh), (2021 model)

Weight:
306 pounds
(139 kg), (2021 model)

Enduro and Dual-Sport Motorcycles

KTM 350 EXC Enduro Motorcycle

Dirt racers love the 350 EXC. A cover on the engine protects it from mud.

Years Made:
2011 to present

Maximum Hp:
45 hp (2018 model)

Top Speed:
85 mph
(137 kmh),
(2018 model)

Weight:
229 pounds
(104 kg), (2018 model)

Suzuki DR-Z400S

Suzuki makes a lot of dual-sport bikes. There is a Suzuki DualSport Riders Club. The club has events all over the United States.

Years Made:
2000 to present

Maximum Hp:
48 hp (2001 model)

Top Speed:
94 mph
(151 kmh), (2001 model)

Weight:
291 pounds
(132 kg), (2001 model)

Enduro and Dual-Sport Motorcycles

Yamaha WR250R

The WR250R is good for experienced and beginning riders. Yamaha worked hard to get the seat just right. It is comfortable both on and off the road.

Years Made:
2008 to 2020

Maximum Hp:
30 hp (2008 model)

Top Speed:
82 mph
(132 kmh),
(2008 model)

Weight:
278 pounds
(126 kg), (2008 model)

Customized off-road motorcycle built for the beach

Did You Know?

Customizing is a way to make a bike special. Owners can change the engine or the handlebars. They can swap out the tires for different ones. A bike can be painted with a design. Each custom bike is unique.

Supermotos

Supermoto racing is different from motocross. In Supermoto races, the speeds are slower. The dirt is smoother. Supermoto races are a mix of flat tracks, motocross, and road racing.

Husqvarna 701 Supermoto

A supermoto, like the Husqvarna 701 Supermoto, is a combination of a dirt bike, a dual-sport motorcycle, and a sports bike. The seats are tall. The handlebars are high.

Years Made:
2015 to present

Maximum Hp:
74 hp (2017 model)

Top Speed:
120 mph
(193 kmh), (2017 model)

Weight:
320 pounds
(145 kg),
(2017 model)

Trials Bikes

Trials bikes are used in off-road competitions. Riders are tested on their balance and skill. They are also tested on stunts. These races are not about speed.

Did You Know?

In trials racing, points are bad! Each time riders touch their feet to the ground, they get a point. If riders don't finish the course, they get five points. It's called a fiasco.

GasGas TXT Pro 250

The GasGas TXT Pro 250 is built to be strong but flexible. But, like all trials bikes, it doesn't have a seat! That makes it better for racing.

Years Made:
2009 to present

Maximum Hp:
25 to 40 hp
(2013 model)

Top Speed:
About 30 mph
(48 kmh), (2023 model)

Weight:
144 pounds
(65 kg), (2013 model)

Street Riders

Road bikes are built to be driven on streets and highways. There are many types of road bikes: bobbers, choppers, cruisers, standards, and tourers.

Ducati XDiavel S

Years Made:
2016 to present

Maximum Hp:
160 hp (2021 model)

Top Speed:
About 150 mph
(241 kmh),
(2021 model)

Weight:
487 pounds
(221 kg),
(2021 model)

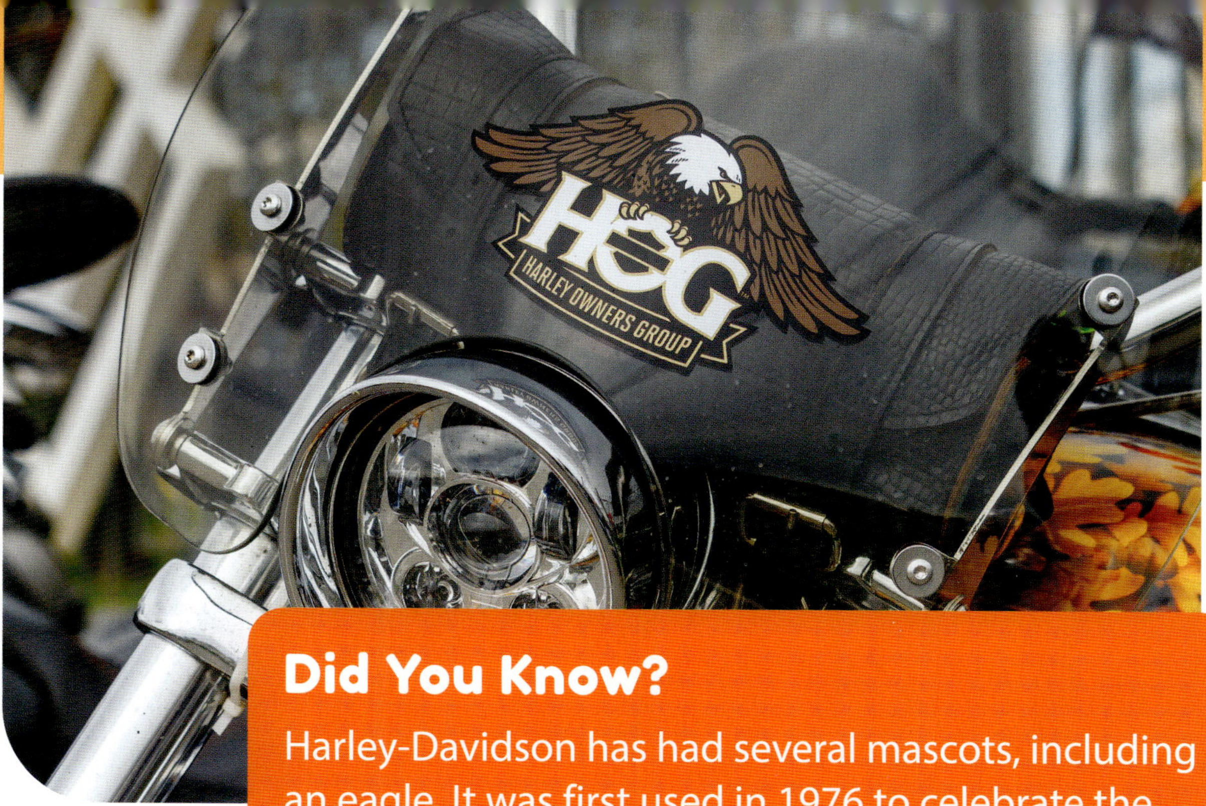

Did You Know?

Harley-Davidson has had several mascots, including an eagle. It was first used in 1976 to celebrate the United States' 200th birthday. But their first mascot was a small pig. That's why a Harley is sometimes called a hog!

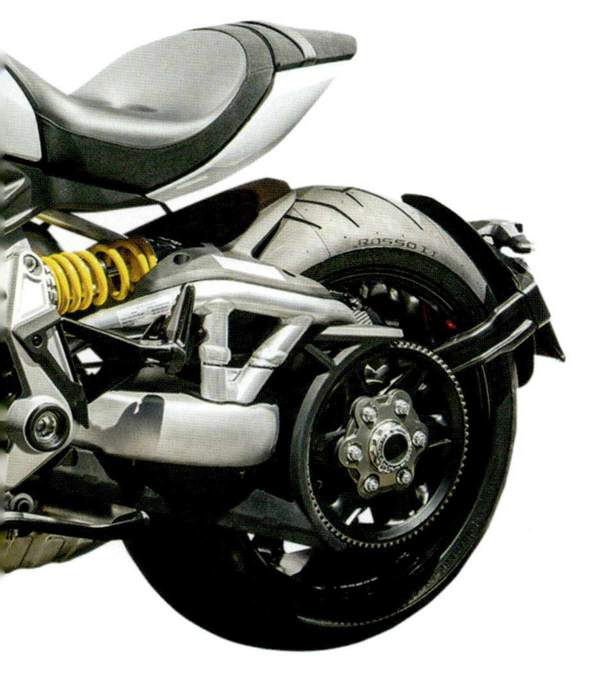

The Ducati XDiavel S is a fast cruiser. Some people choose a bike because of how it looks. Some riders want something fast. Others choose a bike for both speed and style.

Bobbers

Bobbers started off as a way to customize a road bike. Owners would cut or take off extra parts to make their bikes lighter, faster, and drive better. How did the bikes get the name *bobber*? They have shortened, or bobbed, back fenders like a bobtail!

Indian Scout Bobber

The first bobber was built in the 1940s. Bike makers, like Indian, now make bobbers to buy.

Years Made:
2018 to present

Maximum Hp:
100 hp
(2023 model)

Top Speed:
128 mph
(206 kmh), (2023 model)

Weight:
533 pounds
(242 kg), (2023 model)

Triumph Bonneville Bobber

The Triumph Bonneville Bobber has a seat that looks like it's floating. Many early bobbers had seats like this too. That's because some parts underneath were stripped away.

Years Made:
2016 to present

Maximum Hp:
77 hp (2017 model)

Top Speed:
110 mph
(177 kmh), (2017 model)

Weight:
502 pounds
(228 kg), (2017 model)

FUN FACT!

Bobbers used to be called "bob-jobs."

Choppers

The name *chopper* comes from the word *chopped*. Other bikes were "chopped" up and put together to make these bikes.

American IronHorse Texas Chopper

The seat position on choppers, like the American IronHorse Texas chopper, can be hard to get used to. Riders sit low. Their feet are forward, and the handlebars are high.

Year Built:
2006

Maximum Hp:
110 hp

Top Speed:
About 124 mph
(200 kmh)

Weight:
610 pounds
(277 kg)

Big Dog Ridgeback Chopper

Big Dog builds custom motorcycles. They ship them all over the world.

Year Built:
2009

Maximum Hp:
About 98 hp

Top Speed:
About 131 mph
(211 kmh)

Weight:
680 pounds
(308 kg)

FUN FACT!
Choppers are like works of art. No two are alike.

Choppers
Captain America

This Harley-Davidson was a movie star! It was in the movie *Easy Rider*. The bike had an American flag painted on the gas tank. It was called Captain America.

Year This Motorcycle Was Custom Built:
1969

Maximum Hp:
52 hp

Top Speed:
95 mph
(153 kmh)

Weight:
540 pounds
(245 kg)

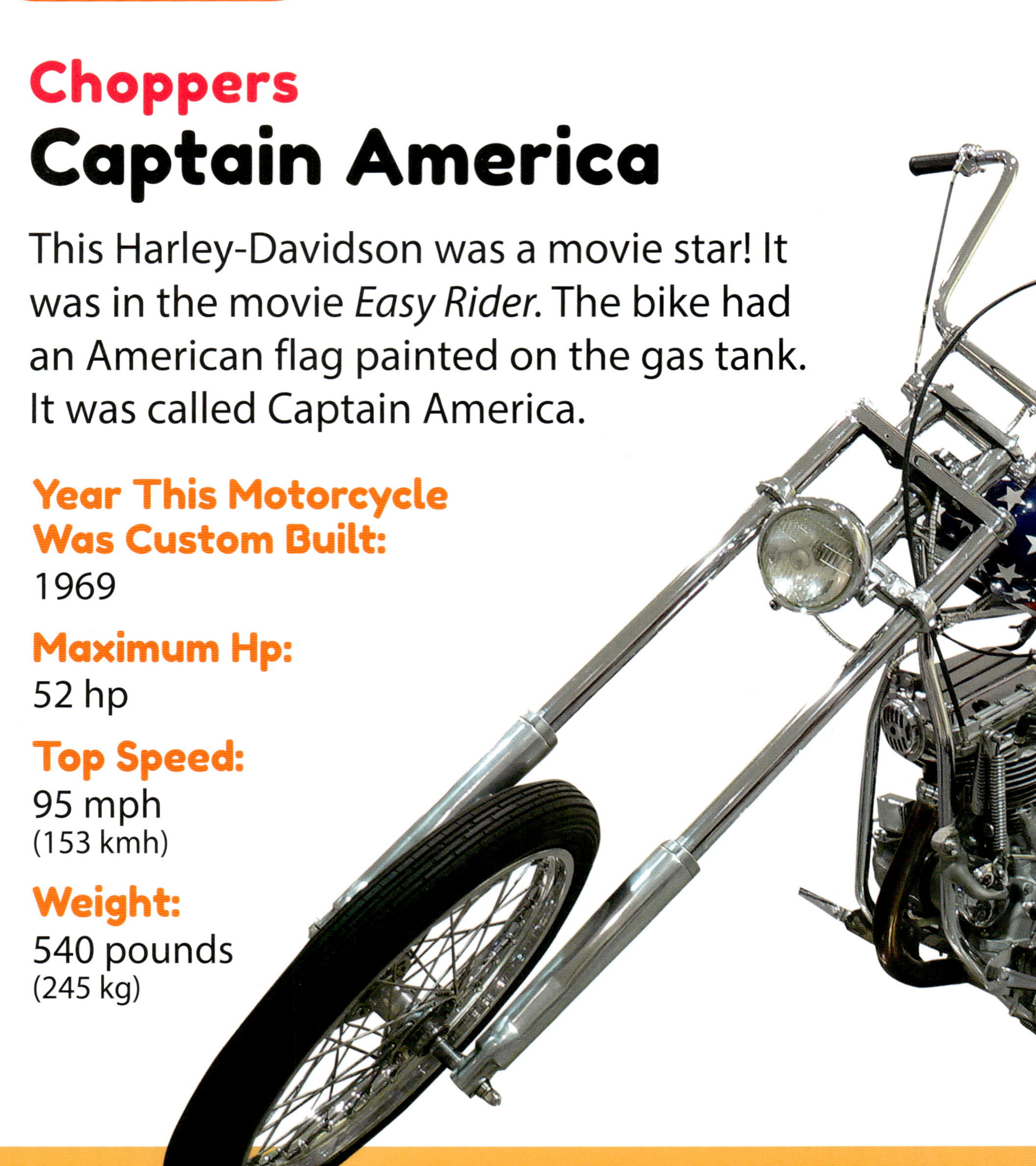

A few Captain America bikes were made for the movie. All except one were stolen immediately after filming.

Did You Know?

Motorcycle Mania and *Monster Garage* were TV shows about choppers. They starred Jesse James. He didn't just chop bikes. He chopped a Ford Mustang into a lawnmower. He also chopped a Lincoln Town Car into a fire truck!

Cruisers

Cruisers are just for what their name says: cruising!

Harley-Davidson History

Harley-Davidson is one of the most popular cruiser brands. The company was started by three Davidson brothers (Arthur, William, and Walter) and William Harley. They grew up together in Milwaukee, Wisconsin.

FUN FACT!

The Harley-Davidson Museum is in Milwaukee, Wisconsin.

In 1903, they made their first motorcycle in a shack! In 1906, they began making motorcycles in a factory. The company grew from there.

Harley-Davidson is now a famous motorcycle company.

Harley-Davidson Fat Boy

The Fat Boy was ridden in the movie *Terminator 2: Judgement Day*.

Years Made:
1989 to present

Maximum Hp:
65 hp (1990 model)

Top Speed:
110 mph
(177 kmh),
(1990 model)

Weight:
690 pounds
(313 kg), (1990
model)

Cruisers

Harley-Davidson Softail Slim

This bike is powerful. It is fast. It's easy to ride. Many think the Softail Slim is the best cruiser Harley-Davidson has ever made.

Years Made:
2012 to 2021

Maximum Hp:
86 hp
(2018 model)

Top Speed:
125 mph
(201 kmh), (2018 model)

Weight:
641 pounds
(291 kg), (2018 model)

Honda CB 750 Four

The Honda CB 750 Four was the first modern cruiser. It came from Japan.

Years Made:
1969 to 2003; 2007

Maximum Hp:
67 hp (1969 model)

Top Speed:
123 mph
(198 kmh), (1969 model)

Weight:
480 pounds
(218 kg), (1969 model)

Honda CMX500 Rebel 500

The Rebel 500 is popular with women, beginners, and shorter riders. It has a low seat. It is easy to handle. It has been made since 2017.

Kawasaki Vulcan 900

The first Vulcan was built in 2006. It was named after the Roman god of fire.

Suzuki M109R B.O.S.S.

This bike was built from 2015 to 2023. People didn't really like it at first. It seemed too modern. It seemed too much like a racer. Over time, people grew to love it.

Yamaha V-Max

The first V-Max was built in 1985. The powerful bike was nicknamed "Mad-Max."

Roadsters

Roadsters are bikes with just the basics. They are lightweight. They are fuel-efficient. Roadsters are smaller than other road bikes. They also cost less.

Roadsters are great for people who live in cities. They don't take up a lot of room.

Yamaha X SR900

The first roadsters came out in the 1950s. They have been popular ever since. Many riders love the retro style.

Years Made:
2016 to present

Maximum Hp:
113 hp
(2019 model)

Top Speed:
150 mph
(241 kmh),
(2019 model)

Weight:
430 pounds
(195 kg),
(2019 model)

Standard Motorcycles

Standard motorcycles are the oldest style of bike. Sitting on one is like sitting on a regular bike. All the major bike makers have standard motorcycles.

Ducati Monster

The Monster was built from parts of other Ducati bikes. The bike was a big hit.

Years Made:
1993 to present

Maximum Hp:
6.5 hp (1998 M900 model)

Top Speed:
121 mph
(195 kmh),
(1998 M900 model)

Weight:
449 pounds
(204 kg), (1998 M900 model)

Honda CB600F Hornet

The Hornet has a lower seat height. That makes it a good choice for short riders.

Years Made:
1998 to 2013

Maximum Hp:
97 hp (2006 model)

Top Speed:
140 mph
(225 kmh), (2006 model)

Weight:
394 pounds
(179 kg), (2006 model)

Standard Motorcycles

Triumph Street Twin

The Street Twin is one of Triumph's best sellers. The bike is easy to ride. It can handle any turn. The seat is comfortable. It's also larger, so a rider can take a passenger.

Years Made:
2016 to present

Maximum Hp:
55 hp (2016 model)

Top Speed:
115 mph
(185 kmh), (2016 model)

Weight:
437 pounds
(198 kg),
(2016 model)

Yamaha XSR900

Years Made:
2016 to present

Maximum Hp:
116 hp (2016 model)

Top Speed:
150 mph
(241 kmh), (2016 model)

Weight:
430 pounds
(195 kg), (2016 model)

The XSR900 has a retro style. It was made to look like old Yamaha bikes. Many riders love this look.

Did You Know?

Some new standard bikes look like classics. Don't let the looks fool you. They have modern technology.

Touring Motorcycles

Touring bikes are for long-distance riding. They have windscreens. The seats are large enough for a passenger.

Touring bikes also have large fuel tanks. Riders can travel farther.

Did You Know?

A top case is like a little trunk. It can be strapped on to the bike. It gives riders extra space for things they need.

BMW R100RS

The BMW R100RS is a mix of a sports bike and a touring motorcycle. The bike can go 100 mph (161 kph) for hours. It won't whine or shake, as other bikes do.

Years Made:
1976 to 1996

Maximum Hp:
70 hp (1977 model)

Top Speed:
125 mph
(201 kmh),
(1977 model)

Weight:
535 pounds
(243 kg), (1977 model)

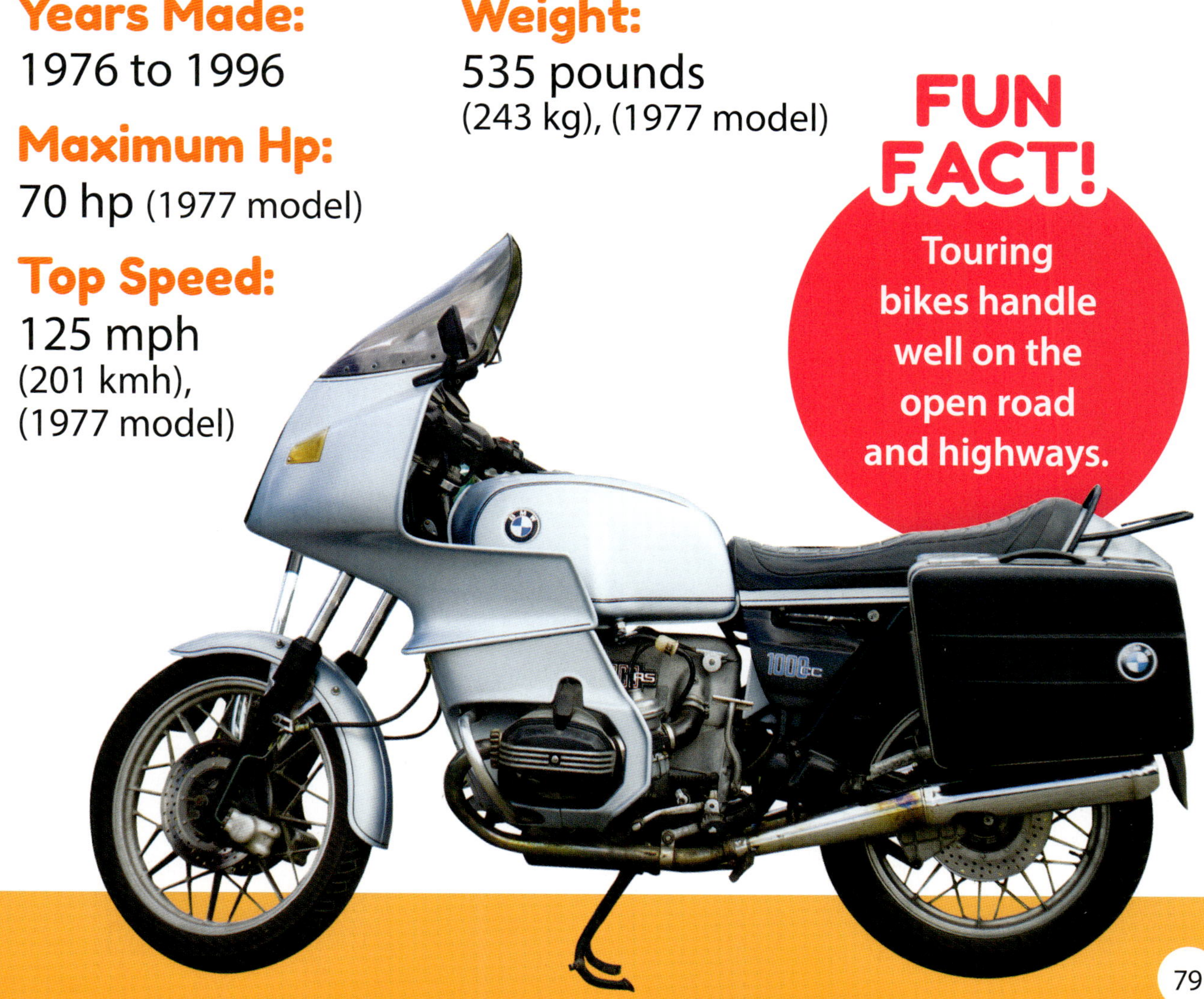

FUN FACT!

Touring bikes handle well on the open road and highways.

Touring Motorcycles

Honda GL1000 Gold Wing

Some people think the Honda Gold Wing is the best touring bike in the world.

Years Made:
1972 to present

Maximum Hp:
81 hp (1974 model)

Top Speed:
125 mph
(201 kmh), (1974 model)

Weight:
584 pounds
(265 kg), (1974 model)

Did You Know?
Touring motorcycles are sometimes called dressers. That's because bikers like to dress up their bikes with extra features like heated seats.

Touring motorcycles often have more safety features. Many also have heated seats. Some have navigation to help riders find their way.

BSA Gold Star

Gold Stars were hand built. This meant owners could make changes to the bikes they were about to buy. This bike was made from 1938 to 1963.

Honda C100 Super Cub

This is one of the most popular bikes Honda has made. The first one was made in 1958. They are still being made today. So far, more than 100 million bikes have been sold.

Indian Chief Vintage

This popular bike looks vintage. But it's not that old. It was built in 2018. It was designed to look like a bike from the past.

Kawasaki Eliminator

This power cruiser was a big hit for Kawasaki. It was built from 1985 to 2007. A newer version was made in 2023.

Motorcycle Gear

Motorcycle riders wear special gear to keep them safe. The most important safety gear is the motorcycle helmet.

The rest of the body also needs protection. Leather gloves protect the rider's hands. A motorcycle jacket protects the upper body. Motorcycle boots provide traction. Leather or Kevlar pants protect the rider's legs.

Did You Know?

Motorcycle riders need a special driver's license.

Tips for Safe Driving

- Take a safety course.
- Check the weather and be prepared.
- Wear motorcycle gear.
- Look over the bike before each ride.
- Make sure other drivers can see you.
- Stay a safe distance away from other vehicles.
- Carry a first-aid kit.
- Don't ride when you are tired.

Getting around Town

Scooters are motorcycles with small engines and wheels. They are light. They turn easily.

Riders don't straddle scooters. They put their feet on riding platforms. Scooters are great for people who live in cities or on college campuses.

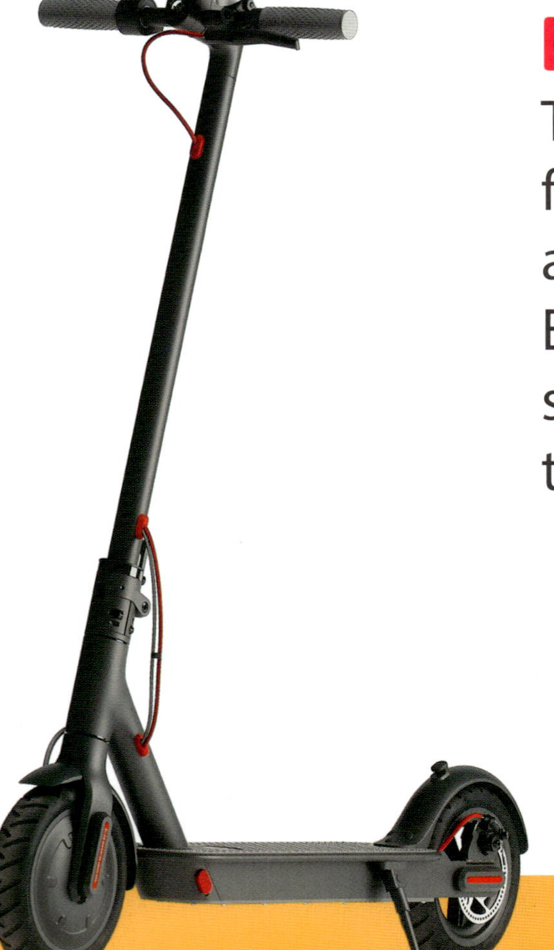

E-Scooters

The *e* in e-Scooters stands for "electric." E-scooters are powered by a battery. E-scooters don't have a seat. The rider stands on the platform.

Did You Know?

Like bike riders, e-scooter riders must follow all traffic laws. Riders must stop at red lights and stop signs.

Many cities have sharing programs. People can pay to take an e-scooter someplace. They can then leave it there.

Mopeds

Mopeds are part bicycle and part motorcycle. Most mopeds have pedals. They also have a small engine. The rider can pedal the moped. The engine can also power the moped. Or both the engine and rider can power it.

Yamaha FS1-E (the Fizzy)

The 1973 Fizzy had a top speed of 60 mph (97 kmh). Later bikes were limited to about 30 mph (48 kmh). This made the bikes safer.

Years Made:
1971 to 1983

Maximum Hp:
4.8 hp (1973 model)

Top Speed:
60 mph
(97 kmh), (1973 model)

Weight:
154 pounds
(70 kg), (1973 model)

Mopeds are great for getting around town. They have good fuel economy. They are good for people who want a little exercise.

Peugeot Metropolis Allure

This scooter has two wheels in the front to make it more stable. Drivers don't need a motorcycle license to drive them. A car license is all that is needed.

Years Made:
2022 to present

Maximum Hp:
35.6 hp (2023 model)

Top Speed:
83 mph
(134 kmh),
(2023 model)

Weight:
564 pounds
(256 kg),
(2023 model)

FUN FACT!

Peugeot, a French company, is the oldest manufacturer of scooters.

Motor Scooters

Scooters are popular in Europe. They are also popular on US college campuses. They are great for traveling too. They can be strapped to the back of an RV or SUV.

Vespare means "to go somewhere on a Vespa."

Motor Scooters

Vespa GTS 300

The first Vespa was built in 1946 in Italy. The word *vespa* means "wasp" in Italian. The maker of the scooter thought it sounded like a wasp. The name stuck!

Years Made:
2009 to present

Maximum Hp:
23.8 hp (2020 model)

Top Speed:
80 mph
(129 kmh), (2020 model)

Weight:
348 pounds
(158 kg), (2020 model)

Did You Know?

Vespas have been in many movies. The 1953 movie *Roman Holiday* made Vespas popular.

BMW CE 04w

The BMW CE 04w is an electric scooter. The first of these scooters was built in 2021. It is a popular scooter for drivers who commute within a city. It has a range of 80 miles (129 km) on a single charge.

Kymco AK550

Kymco is a motorcycle maker from Taiwan. The first AK550 was built in 2016. It has a low center of gravity. That makes it have better handling.

Piaggio X7 250

Piaggio is the same Italian company that makes Vespas. The first X7 250 scooter was built in 2008.

SYM Mio

The SYM Mio is a moped, which means it can park where bicycles park—in a bike rack. That makes this moped popular with people who live in areas with limited parking.

Delivery Bikes

Many companies use motorcycles to deliver goods. Bikes are less expensive than cars or trucks. Bikes can move quickly through crowded streets. They use less gas. This saves money. Most bikes can be turned into delivery motorcycles. An attachment is added to carry the goods.

Harley-Davidson Servi-Car

Many businesses used Servi-Cars. Car repair shops used them. When a car was fixed, it was attached to the Servi-Car. It was towed to the owner's house. The car was unhooked. Then the repairman rode the bike back to the shop.

Years Made:
1932 to 1973

Maximum Hp:
24 hp (1952 model)

Top Speed:
63 mph
(101 kmh), (1952 model)

Weight:
600 pounds
(272 kg), (1952 model)

Electric Trike Bicycles

Electric trike bicycles, or e-trikes, look like giant tricycles. E-trikes are battery powered. The rider can also pedal to power the bike. That makes e-trikes better for the environment. Riding an e-trike can be good exercise.

FUN FACT!

In many states, you must be 18 years old to ride an e-trike.

Did You Know?

The electric tricycle was invented in 1881 in France. Back then, people rode in carriages pulled by horses. The tricycles scared the horses. Some horses reared up and ran. E-trike riders had to pull over to let the horses pass.

Enclosed Motorcycles

An enclosed motorcycle looks like a tiny car. The rider sits inside.

Some enclosed bikes have three wheels. Others have two. These bikes have "landing gear." Two tiny wheels drop to the ground when the bike is stopped. This way, the bike won't fall over.

FUN FACT!

Enclosed motorcycles can protect riders from the weather.

Carver One

In 1997, the police drove a test model of the Carver One in the Netherlands. They made sure it was safe before it was sold.

Years Made:
2007 to 2009

Maximum Hp:
68 hp (2007 model)

Top Speed:
115 mph
(185 kmh), (2007 model)

Weight:
1,477 pounds
(670 kg), (2007 model)

Police, Fire, and Ambulance Motorcycles

Many rescue workers and police officers use motorcycles. The bikes have special features. They have windscreens and saddle boxes. They have lights that flash. They also have radios and sirens. Motorcycles can move easily through crowds. They can reach an accident more quickly than a car can.

Did You Know?

Some people use motorcycles to carry goods to hospitals. They carry blood and other supplies.

BMW F800GS

A special version of the BMW F800GS was built for firefighting. It has two tanks. They hold a mixture of water and foam to put out fires.

Years Made:
2008 to 2018

Maximum Hp:
85 hp (2009 model)

Top Speed:
124 mph
(200 kmh), (2009 model)

Weight:
392 pounds
(178 kg), (2009 model)

Did You Know?

In 2009, Austin, Texas, created a program that uses motorcycles. Paramedics and others can drive to patients. This makes it easier for people to get medical care.

BMW R 1200 RT

This bike is made for paramedics. It has a flashing light on the back. It also has speakers. There are large saddle boxes to carry equipment. An extra battery powers electrical rescue equipment.

Years Made:
2005 to 2019

Maximum Hp:
109.8 hp
(2015 model for medics)

Top Speed:
145 mph
(233 kmh),
(2015 model for medics)

Weight:
604 pounds
(274 kg),
(2015 nonmedic)

Harley-Davidson FLHTP Electra Glide

The US Secret Service rides in presidential motorcades. They have been using Harley-Davidsons since July 2001.

Years Made:
1983 to present

Maximum Hp:
92.5 hp (2021 model)

Top Speed:
99 mph
(159 kmh), (2021 model)

Weight:
809 pounds
(367 kg), (2021 model)

Harley-Davidson Police Road King

Harley-Davidson has been making police bikes for more than 115 years. Some motorcycle officers wear a special symbol on their uniform. It's a winged wheel. The wings are symbols of speed.

Did You Know?

In 1910, Chicago added 12 motorcycle police officers to catch speeders. The newspaper called these officers iron horse policemen.

Years Made:
1994 to present

Maximum Hp:
100.5 hp (2022 model)

Top Speed:
108 mph
(174 kmh), (2022 model)

Weight:
794 pounds
(360 kg), (2022 model)

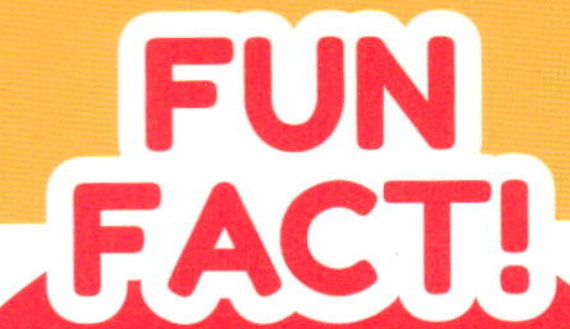

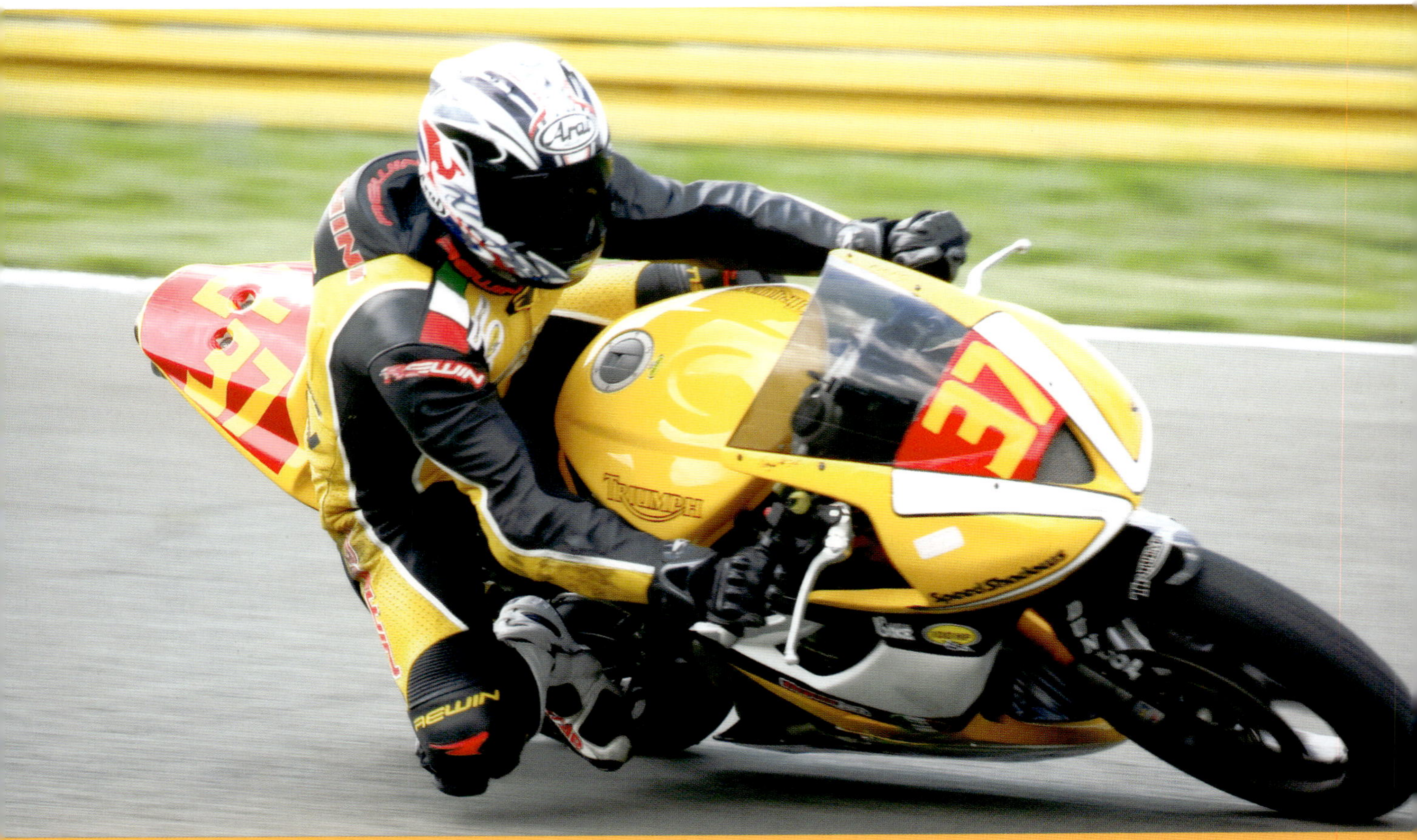

Built for Speed

Sports motorcycles are built for racing. Riders choose their bikes based on the type of race. Café racers are often customized. Minibikes are small. Streetfighters are fast and have a low grumble. Some say they sound mean!

FUN FACT!

People can buy a ticket to drive a lap around the Daytona Speedway track!

Did You Know?

The Daytona 200 race is popular. The race was first held on the beach in Daytona, Florida, in 1937. Now it's held at the Daytona International Speedway. The race is 200 miles (322 km) long.

Café Racers

Café racers are customized bikes. Owners take off any parts they don't need. That makes the bikes lighter and faster.

Did You Know?

Café racing began in the United Kingdom in the 1950s. People who wanted to race met in cafés. They planned street races at their meetings. This is how the bike got its name.

Ducati Scrambler Café Racer

Riders were confused by the name of this bike at first. How was it a scrambler *and* a café racer? Scrambler was just the bike's name. But the type of bike was a café racer.

Years Made:
2017 to present

Maximum Hp:
73 hp
(2021 model)

Top Speed:
130 mph
(209 kmh),
(2021 model)

Weight:
397 pounds
(180 kg), (2021 model)

Café Racers

Norton Commando 961 Café Racer

This bike was designed to look like the first Norton Commando from the 1960s. But the 961 has modern technology. Parts of it are hand built. It costs a lot of money. Many believe the price is worth it.

Years Made:
2010 to present

Maximum Hp:
80 hp (2010 model)

Top Speed:
130 mph
(209 kmh),
(2010 model)

Weight:
415 pounds
(188 kg), (2010 model)

FUN FACT!

The 961 Café Racer was based on the famous Norton Commando, first built in 1967.

Triumph Thruxton 1200 R

The style of café racers has changed. Today, many bikes, like the Triumph Thruxton, are called café racers.

Years Made:
2015 to 2020

Maximum Hp:
97 hp (2018 model)

Top Speed:
135 mph
(217 kmh), (2018 model)

Weight:
448 pounds
(203 kg), (2018 model)

Hypersports Bikes

Hypersports bikes are bigger, longer, and heavier. They are also much faster. They are aerodynamic. Their engines have more power than sports bikes.

Kawasaki Ninja H2

The racing version of this bike is the fastest bike a person can buy. But it is illegal, or against the law, to drive the racing version on the street.

Years Made:
2015 to present

Maximum Hp:
200 hp (2015 model)

Top Speed:
187 mph
(301 kmh), (2015 model)

Weight:
525 pounds
(238 kg), (2015 model)

Suzuki Hayabusa (Busa)

This bike was inspired by the peregrine falcon, the world's fastest animal.

Years Made:
1999 to present

Maximum Hp:
195.7 hp (2014 model)

Top Speed:
185.5 mph
(299 kmh), (2014 model)

Weight:
485 pounds
(220 kg), (2014 model)

FUN FACT!

When diving, a peregrine falcon can reach speeds up to 240 mph (386 kmh)!

Minibikes

A minibike is like a cross between a scooter and a motorcycle. They're about the size of a scooter. But they have all the parts of a full-sized motorcycle. Riders race minibikes for fun. They are faster than a go-cart. They cost less and are easy to carry. They're also easy to take care of.

Did You Know?

"Grom" is a nickname for a young surfer. American Honda Motor is in Southern California. Southern California is home to lots of young surfers!

Honda Grom

The Grom was an instant hit. Dealers couldn't keep them in their stores. People began customizing the bikes. Clubs and races formed around the Grom.

Years Made:
2013 to present

Maximum Hp:
9.7 hp (2018 model)

Top Speed:
73 mph
(117 kmh), (2018 model)

Weight:
229 pounds
(104 kg), (2018 model)

Minibikes
Honda Monkey

In the late 1970s, the Monkey was popular with RV (recreational vehicle) drivers. It was easy to strap it to the RV. People could take the bike on trips. And it was fun to ride.

The first Honda Monkey was part of an amusement park ride. It became so popular they made one for the street!

Did You Know?

Pit minibikes are mini dirt bikes. They were first used in motocross races. Workers rode these small bikes in the pits. Racers go to pit areas to get gas or change tires. Now people race pit bikes!

Years Made:
1963 to 2017

Maximum Hp:
3.62 hp (2017 model)

Top Speed:
25 mph
(40 kmh), (2017 model)

Weight:
150 pounds
(68 kg), (2017 model)

Streetfighters

Bikers liked to race and do tricks. They often crashed. Replacing all the damaged parts was expensive. So, they started removing parts. They took off anything that wasn't necessary. The bikes became known as streetfighters.

FUN FACT!

Streetfighters have engines with a low and loud grumble. They sound mean—like fighters. That's how they got their name.

KTM 390 Duke

The KTM 390 Duke is a great bike for beginners. It's lightweight, so it's easy to handle. It's also good for learning tricks. It performs well on highways. It's fast on the race track.

Years Made:
2012 to present

Maximum Horsepower:
43.5 hp (2019 model)

Top Speed:
106 mph
(171 kmh), (2019 model)

Weight:
328 pounds
(149 kg), (2019 model)

Streetfighters

Streetfighters were first made by the riders themselves. They would take parts off of a bike. They would turn the bike into a streetfighter. In the 1990s, motorcycle companies began making factory streetfighters. This means the bikes came looking like a streetfighter already.

Did You Know?

Bikers are allowed to ride streetfighters on the road. However, riders can get tired easily. Streetfighters don't have wind protection. Most riders don't buy streetfighters for long rides.

Triumph Speed Triple S/RS

One of the first factory streetfighters was the 1994 Triumph Speed Triple S/RS.

Years Made:
1994 to present

Maximum Hp:
147.9 hp (2020 model)

Top Speed:
150 mph
(241 kmh), (2020 model)

Weight:
423 pounds
(192 kg), (2020 model)

BMW R nineT Café Racer

This bike was first made in 2014. The name nineT means "90." BMW was 90 years old when the bike was made.

Ducati 916

Ducati is a leading motorcycle maker. This bike was made from 1994 to 1998. It has won four Superbike World Championships.

Honda VTR1000 SP2

This sports motorcycle was made from 2000 to 2007. Honda was tired of losing the Superbike World Championship to Ducati. They created this bike to challenge the Ducati 916. In 2000, the Honda VTR1000 won the World Superbike title. But Ducati reclaimed the title in 2001.

Yamaha MT-07

The MT-07 is popular. Riders like the way it looks and sounds. It also costs less than most streetfighters.

GLOSSARY

aerodynamic
Describes a bike that can go faster because the air isn't slowing it down.

competition
A contest in which motorcyclists are judged to see who is the best.

customize
To build or change something to make it special.

fuel-efficient
Describes an engine that uses less fuel.

ground clearance
The open space between the bottom of the bike and the ground.

monoshock
A part of a bike that creates fewer bumps, fewer vibrations, and less noise for the rider.

off-road
Describes driving on roads that are not paved.

traction
Grip on the surface of an object, like a tire or a shoe, that makes it less slippery.

windscreen
The glass on the front of a bike that protects the rider from the wind.

More Books to Read

Bold Kids. *Motorcycles: Children's Transportation Book*. Bold Books, 2022.

Huddleston, Emma. *Start Your Engines! Motocross Cycles*. Kaleidoscope, 2019.

Marcos, Victoria. *My Favorite Machine: Motorcycles*. Xist Publishing, 2021.

Online Resources

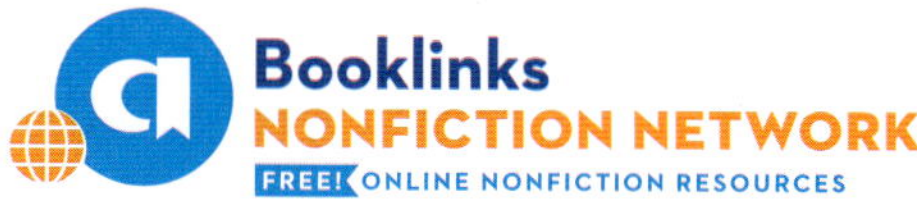

To learn more about motorcycles, please visit **abdobooklinks.com** or scan this QR code. These links are routinely monitored and updated to provide the most current information available.

INDEX

PHOTO CREDITS

Cover Photos: citybrabus/Shutterstock Images, front (Suzuki); DJ Srki/Shutterstock Images, front (background); Heritage Images/Getty Images, front (Harley-Davidson); Sunflower Momma/Shutterstock Images, front (Indian); Charlesimage/Shutterstock Images, back (Vespa)

Interior Photos: KTM AG/Marlon Ötzi/Wikimedia Commons, 1, 55; milovad/Shutterstock Images, 4 (top); Kamin Jaroensuk/Shutterstock Images, 4 (bottom); Mr. Crocodile/Shutterstock Images, 5, 60; Vasily Timofeev/Dreamstime.com, 6–7; Illustrated London News/Stringer/Getty Images, 8 (top); SOPA Images/Getty Images, 8 (middle), 31 (top), 74; Bettmann/Getty Images, 8 (bottom); Scott Olson/Staff/Getty Images, 9 (top); Steve Glover/Flickr Commons, 9 (bottom); Stahlkocher/Wikimedia Commons, 11; Dmitriy Feldman/Dreamstime.com, 13; DEA/G. Cigolini/Getty Images, 14; Freddy Dendoktoor/Public Domain Pictures, 15; Keystone/Stringer/Getty Images, 16; Mike Schinkel/Flickr Commons, 17 (top); David Ashdown/Stringer/Getty Images, 17 (bottom); Clari Massimiliano/Shutterstock Images, 18; Richard B. Levine/Newscom, 19 (top); Kobac/Wikimedia Commons, 19 (bottom); Thomas Vogt/Wikimedia Commons, 20; Stig Alenas/Shutterstock Images, 21; Fox Photos/Getty Images, 22; Yesterdays Antique Motorcycles/Wikimedia Commons, 23 (top); Ian Walton/Getty Images, 23 (bottom); Dan Callister/Getty Images, 24; Joachim Köhler/Wikimedia Commons, 25, 64; Photoshot/Newscom, 26; ウェルワイ/Wikimedia Commons, 28 (top); Tony Hisgett/Flickr Commons, 28 (bottom); Heritage Images/Getty Images, 29 (top), 67, 124 (bottom); The Enthusiast Network/Getty Images, 29 (bottom); sylv1rob1/Shutterstock Images, 30; Elis Cora/Getty Images, 31 (bottom); Jarretera/Getty Images, 33; Anadolu Agency/Getty Images, 34, 94 (top); Rattanachai Singtrangarn/Dreamstime.com, 35; Anatoliy Lukich/Shutterstock Images, 36; Ryan Urlacher/Wikimedia Commons, 37; Suwin/Shutterstock Images, 38; Eric Bery/Shutterstock Images, 39; Daniel Hartwig/Flickr Commons, 40 (top); Priwo/Wikimedia Commons, 40 (bottom); Picture Alliance/Getty Images, 41; Maciej Kopaniecki/Shutterstock Images, 42; Edu2ev/Shutterstock Images, 43; Betto Rodrigues/Shutterstock Images, 44–45; Dylanr132/Dreamstime.com, 46; Rainmaker47/Wikimedia Commons, 47; Haryanta Prih/Shutterstock Images, 48; Chanokchon/Wikimedia Commons, 49, 70 (top); Evren Kalinbacak/Dreamstime.com, 50; Betto Rodrigues/Shutterstock Images, 51; Vincenzo Lombardo/Stringer/Getty Images, 52; Aleksandr Korchagin/Dreamstime.com, 53; OlegRi/Shutterstock Images, 54, 109 (bottom); xuanhuongho/Shutterstock Images, 56; Y Sekiai/Wikimedia Commons, 57 (top); Suvorov_Alex/Shutterstock Images, 57 (bottom); Grzegorz Czapski/Shutterstock Images, 58; Vladimir Zhupanenko/Shutterstock Images, 59; Alex Tanchoco/Wikimedia Commons, 61; Ashley Cooper/Alamy Stock Photo, 62; Ingolf Kühn/David Harex/Wikimedia Commons, 63; Joe Seer/Shutterstock Images, 65; Sayar Tholib/Shutterstock Images, 66 (top); Wisconsinart/Dreamstime.com, 66 (bottom); Nitot/Wikimedia Commons, 68; gianlucacolagrossi/Getty Images, 69; OSX/order_242/Wikimedia Commons, 70 (bottom); Steve Lagreca/Getty Images, 71 (top), 107 (bottom); vuk8691/Getty Images, 71 (bottom); Sound Media/Public Domain Pictures, 72–73; Nogard13/PekePON/Wikimedia Commons, 75; Marc Pfitzenreuter/Getty Images, 76; O1dm0n/Wikimedia Commons, 77; Anze Furlan/Dreamstime.com, 78; Sergey Kohl/Shutterstock Images, 79; sadicarnot/Wikimedia Commons, 81; Jhernan124/Dreamstime.com, 82 (top); Kyodo/Newscom, 82 (bottom); 玄史生/Wikimedia Commons, 83 (top); Museo8bits/Wikimedia Commons, 83 (bottom); Louie Schoeman/Shutterstock Images, 84; U.S. Navy photo/Deris Jeannette/Wikimedia Commons, 85; Kostsov/Shutterstock Images, 86; Gary Hershorn/Getty Images, 87; SG2012/Wikimedia Commons, 89; Thesupermat/Wikimedia Commons, 90; Ross Shaw/Dreamstime.com, 91; Golf Standard/Shutterstock Images, 92; Silvano Audisio/Shutterstock Images, 93 (top); John Springer Collection/Getty Images, 93 (bottom); Laura Buononome/Corvettec6r/Wikimedia Commons, 94 (bottom); Chris Baird/Wikimedia Commons, 95 (top); Ildar Sagdejev/Wikimedia Commons, 95 (bottom); Ideal Classic Cars/Wikimedia Commons, 97; Golden Shrimp/Shutterstock Images, 98; Raoul Marquis/Wikimedia Commons, 99 (top); macondo/Shutterstock Images, 99 (bottom); Ifeelstock/Dreamstime.com, 100; Andrew Balcombe/Shutterstock Images, 101; rightclickstudios/Shutterstock Images, 102; G0d4ather/Dreamstime.com, 103; Andrew Harker/Shutterstock Images, 104; Elvert Barnes/FlickrCommons, 105; REDA&CO/Getty Images, 106; Underwood Archives/Getty Images, 107 (bottom); Lario Tus/Shutterstock Images, 108; Icon Sports Wire/Getty Images, 109 (top); Vereshchagin Dmitry/Shutterstock Images, 110; Nikkolia/Shutterstock Images, 111; Richard-7/Getty Images, 112; 22tomtom/Dreamstime.com, 113; Brphoto/Dreamstime.com, 114; Chatchai Somwat/Dreamstime.com, 115; Andrea Leone/Shutterstock Images, 116; Louis Welsh/Dreamstime.com, 117; Pedro Monteiro/Shutterstock Images, 118; Ovu0ng/Shutterstock Images, 119; Sklo Studio/Shutterstock Images, 120; AnithamRaju Yaragorla/Shutterstock Images, 121; Bartlomiej Kopczynski/Dreamstime.com, 122–123; Konstantinos Moraitis/Dreamstime.com, 124 (top); Rikita/Wikimedia Commons, 125 (top); Sylvain Robin/Dreamstime.com, 125 (bottom)